revealed

Experiencing God's Authentic Love

Kerry Clarensau

and Jodi Detrick, Joanna Weaver, Janelle Hail, JoAnn Butrin

∴ Influence

Influence

www.InfluenceResources.com

Published by Influence Resources
1445 N. Boonville Ave., Springfield, Missouri 65802

Published in association with The Quadrivium Group—Orlando, FL
info@TheQuadriviumGroup.com
and New Vantage Partners—Franklin, TN
info@NewVantagePartners.net

Cover design by Archetype Brands—Springfield, MO
Interior design and typesetting by Wellspring Design and Jay Victor—Nashville, TN

ISBN: 978-1-936699-09-4

First printing 2011

Printed in United States of America

love
revealed

dedication

This book is dedicated to every woman who will be served by Convoy of Hope and the National Breast Cancer Foundation.

contents

acknowledgements

Thank you to the women who have revealed God's love through the pages of this book, but most importantly in your daily decisions.

To Jodi Detrick, for times of encouragement through meaningful conversations, you truly show authentic love to everyone you meet. To Janelle Hail, for passionately living a life of service to women across the world struggling with breast cancer. To Joanna Weaver, for obediently writing the words in your books that have inspired me; I count them a treasure. To JoAnn Butrin, for faithfully serving those around you and being a living example of God's extravagant love.

preface

A few months after my husband and I became pastors in Wichita, I was sitting in my office feeling completely overwhelmed. My kids were struggling to adjust to their new schools and youth group. I missed my friends, my home, and the work I left behind. But even more than the adjustments or homesickness, I was actually questioning if God had led us to this place, or if we made a *huge* mistake!

All morning, the lump in my throat was on the verge of giving way to a blubbering mess of tears. Questions consumed my thoughts. *Lord, is this really where you want us? What about my kids? Is it supposed to be this hard for them? Do I even know how to be a pastor's wife? I feel so inadequate!*

Sitting there in the middle of one of the biggest pity parties I've ever thrown (and unfortunately, I've thrown a few), Carol walked into my office with a beautiful bouquet of flowers. She said, "Kerry, I've been thinking about you all morning. And I felt like I was supposed to bring you flowers and tell you that I am so glad you and Mike are our pastors! I don't know how we would have made it through the past couple of months if you weren't here. I just know that God has brought your family to our church!" She hugged me, kissed me on the cheek, and quietly walked out of our office.

I lovingly refer to this experience as the day God sent me flowers. Only God knew the questions and the pain in my heart. And He cared enough to reveal His love through a friend with kind words and a simple gift. It meant more than I can say.

Many people are recipients of God's love through my friend, Carol. She is a beautiful picture of His love, and it is evident in everything she does. She isn't well-known, doesn't have a long list of degrees, or hold a high-powered position. But God's love is revealed every time she calms a crying baby in the nursery, explains a simple truth to a student in her Sunday school class, or rearranges her schedule to care for one of her grandchildren.

Time after time, I've watched Carol make sacrifices for those who were hurting. She gave hours to help a senior adult who lives alone and has difficulty with many household tasks. Carol spent time with lonely women, helping them experience God's love and apply His Truth to their situations. And many times, I've witnessed her sharing resources with those who were struggling financially. God actively loves so many people through this precious friend. And I feel blessed to be one of them!

Through the years I watched her grieve with those who lost loved ones—attending funerals, organizing meals, and spending time with them as they wept. I saw her rejoicing with new moms, brides, graduates.... It was always so much fun to tell her about something exciting going on in my life—her response left no doubt that she was rejoicing with me!

Carol's sacrificial love has taught me many lessons—too many to recount in this limited space. But recently she was helping an expectant mom. This young woman was staying in a hotel close to the hospital due to the serious health issues of her unborn child. Her husband and small child lived several hours away, and she was alone in town without a car. Carol joyfully took her to shop for groceries, to church, and to appointments. And she invited her into her home for warm meals.

One evening I met the expectant mom, and she wept with appreciation as she told me what Carol was doing for her. She said, "I never dreamed someone could be so caring! I really don't know what I would do without her right now."

In so many ways, Carol taught me what it is like to love authentically. I'm thankful for her example and the examples of many other women who have demonstrated the power of God's love—showing me how to accept and reveal God's love.

Love Revealed is a compilation of personal stories by Jodi Detrick, Joanna Weaver, Janelle Hail, JoAnn Butrin, and me. I count it a privilege to call these inspiring women my friends. My prayer is for you to experience God's love in memorable ways as you read their stories and apply God's timeless truths to your life.

Each of the six chapters includes the author's story, Scripture points, talk points, journal points, action points, and prayer points. These are designed to help you understand the biblical principles represented in each story. *Love Revealed* can be completed on your own, but your experience will be much richer if you take this journey with a friend or in a small group. I know you will be encouraged to allow His love to pour through you!

After you've completed *Love Revealed,* ask yourself: How will I allow God to reveal His love through me? This study has a companion 45-day challenge to help you answer this very important question. God may prompt you to take flowers and an encouraging word to a friend, or He may show you the many ways He loves you. *The Love Revealed Challenge* is designed to help you experience God's love and reveal it to others in practical ways. Each day has a Scripture point, thought point, and a practical challenge point. You can take the challenge alone as a devotional, with a friend, or even in a small group. It will be exciting to see what happens as we intentionally accept and reveal God's love!

Kerry Clarensau

Springfield, Missouri

CHAPTER I
love revealed

Kerry Clarensau

"What great love the Father has
lavished on us!" (I John 3:I, NIV)

Don't you just love newborn babies? Every time I look at one, I see God's creative abilities. Everything about them is simply amazing—their little toes, ears, and lips! For days after Tyler, our first son, was born I couldn't take my eyes off him. I would stare at him for hours. I wanted to memorize everything about him. He was simply adorable!

When he was four weeks old, I took him for his first well-baby checkup. I thought I had the most perfect baby in the world, so the idea something could be wrong never entered my mind. My only thought was, *I can't wait to see how much he's grown!*

The first part of the appointment was very routine. The doctor weighed and measured his little body, listened to his heart, looked in his ears and eyes. Everything looked good.

If you have ever watched a pediatrician with a newborn, you have seen him grab the baby's legs below the knees and bend them up in circular motions. I had no idea why the doctor did this, but I watched as he did it several times. And each time he looked a little more concerned.

Finally, he told me that he would like to take some x-rays of Tyler's hips and have an orthopedic specialist look at them. My heart began to beat out of my chest. *What could possibly be wrong? Why do they need to take x-rays of a four-week-old baby?* I suddenly wished my husband, Mike, had taken off work for this appointment.

After reading the x-rays, the pediatrician and the orthopedic specialist came into the exam room with a tiny hip brace and began using words I'd never heard. These words changed our world and soon became a part of our everyday vocabulary. "Your son has congenital hip dysplasia. It is rather severe. If this condition isn't corrected, he will never be able to walk normally. Even with correction, he will probably never be able to run or play sports. He needs to wear this brace 24 hours a day. If his hips don't respond to the brace, we will have to put him in a full-body cast. He might need surgeries in the future, but we will cross that bridge when we come to it."

It's hard to describe how I felt in that moment. The emotions were so overwhelming—I could hardly hear the doctor's words over the sound of my heart beating.

It was surreal to watch the doctor slide the brace under my baby's bottom. He gently lifted each leg into the little harness. He secured Tyler's legs with Velcro straps, positioning his legs at right angles to his body. It looked so uncomfortable!

Tears poured down my cheeks. I struggled to pay attention as the doctor showed me how to take the brace off and walked me through putting it back on. I numbly signed papers and set up the next appointments.

As we walked to our car, I was so heartbroken that I distractedly unlocked the door, threw my bags and keys in, fastened Tyler's car seat, and shut the door. I didn't realize I had locked myself out, until I saw my keys lying on the seat! There I stood on the outside of the car—crying! Almost immediately, Tyler started crying. *What had I done? My poor baby is crying, and I can't get to him!* I'm sure we were quite a sight!

It makes me smile now, but in that moment I was so thankful for a kind woman who volunteered to walk back in the building and call the police to come unlock my car. (This was long before cell phones or OnStar.) We were having a terrible, horrible, no good, very bad day!

On the way home, I drove to Mike's workplace and told him the news. I don't think I will ever forget the look on his face. I knew his dreams of playing baseball with our son felt shattered. We were both so devastated.

That afternoon, all I wanted to do was hold Tyler. It was such an adjustment cuddling a baby in a brace! But we finally settled into the rocking chair. He quickly fell asleep, but I didn't want to put him down. I just held him and cried and prayed like never before. With all of my heart I wanted to take this pain from Tyler. I remember asking God to give my healthy hips and legs to Tyler—I would gladly take his crippled ones. I loved this precious baby so much!

In a quiet moment, God spoke something clearly to my heart. He said, "Kerry, I love Tyler even more than you love him." *How can that be?* I knew how much I loved Tyler; how could He love him more? I would have given anything to take this suffering from him. But this loving God—who knows everything and is all-powerful—asked me to trust Him.

An indescribable peace began to wash over me. And then God spoke something else to my heart, something that changed my relationship with Him forever. He said, "Kerry, I love you—more than you love Tyler." Wow!

I thought about what Jesus had done for me. Just as I wanted to take Tyler's place, He truly took my place. He suffered and died for my sins, so I wouldn't have to. God understood exactly how I was feeling. He loved me so much that He was willing to allow His only Son to suffer for me. I can't explain the peace that washed over me. Suddenly, in the middle of my pain, I gained a new understanding of the depth of His love for me!

God is so good to speak to us! I believe He was preparing my heart earlier that week in my quiet time, when I read King David's words in Psalm 27, verse 10: "Though my father and mother forsake me, the LORD will receive me." David enjoyed a close relationship with God and understood the depths of His love for him. God also spoke through the Old Testament prophet Isaiah saying, "Can a mother forget the infant at her breast, walk away from the baby she bore? But even if mothers forget, I'd never forget you—never" (Isaiah 49:15, THE MESSAGE). God wants us to know that His love for us is even purer and more encompassing than the love of a mother for her newborn child!

Tyler was in either braces or a full-body cast until he was about 24 months old. He was also diagnosed with another type of dysplasia at age five and had several surgeries as a teenager.

Our second son, Blake, was diagnosed with the same condition when he was only six hours old. It was heartbreaking to take him home from the hospital in a brace! He spent eight months in a full-body cast. But thankfully, Blake didn't require any further treatment after he was 14 months old.

While I still wish my boys didn't have dysplasia, I will always be grateful for the lessons our family learned through the journey. God continued to reveal His amazing love every step of the way. Sometimes He demonstrated His love with just enough strength for the moment. Other times He brought caring people to lend a hand. Once, He brought a miraculous healing to Tyler after months of swelling and pain from a surgery.

Just today as I write this chapter, Tyler, a husband and new dad, completed a 5K run—an accomplishment at one time we wouldn't have thought possible. Over the years, Mike and I have quietly celebrated at every baseball, soccer, and basketball game Tyler played.

We can be confident that God wants to reveal His love for each of us in personal ways! We are all unique individuals. As a mom, I grew to understand that my boys receive love differently. I knew Blake needed hugs and attention. And Tyler needed space and words of affirmation. God knows us even more intimately. We can trust Him to reveal His love for us in a unique, meaningful way.

He may speak to you through His Word, in quiet moments of prayer, walking in nature, or through the kindness of a stranger. While your experience will not be like mine, His love for you is just as great!

Understanding His love builds our trust! I learned this firsthand. From that moment in my rocking chair, I've known God loves me. He loves Tyler and Blake. He loves our family. And I can trust His love, even when I don't like or understand my circumstances. As I've depended on Him, I've experienced the joy of His presence in my most difficult moments.

I believe with all of my heart that God wants you to know the full extent of His love! May you grow more and more aware of the revelations of His love!

He wants you to experience authentic love through connections with others. He wants you to grow and mature by encountering His transforming love. He wants to reveal His love in motion as you serve others. He wants the world to see His extravagant love as you care for those in need. And when you are consumed with His love, you can live every moment in the fullness of His presence and experience the joy only He can give.

Scripture Points

Consider how the following verses describe God's love for you:

♥ Psalm 32:10, NIV
Many are the woes of the wicked, but the LORD's unfailing love surrounds the man who trusts in him.

♥ Psalm 36:5-10, NIV
Your love, O LORD, reaches to the heavens, your faithfulness to the skies.

Your righteousness is like the mighty mountains, your justice like the great deep.

O LORD, you preserve both man and beast. How priceless is your unfailing love!

Both high and low among men find refuge in the shadow of your wings.

They feast on the abundance of your house; you give them drink from your river of delights. For with you is the fountain of life; in your light we see light. Continue your love to those who know you, your righteousness to the upright in heart.

♥ Psalm 86:5, 15, NIV
You, Lord, are forgiving and good, abounding in love to all who call to you.... But you, Lord, are a compassionate and gracious God, slow to anger, abounding in love and faithfulness.

♥ Psalm 103:8, 11, 13
The LORD is compassionate and gracious, slow to anger, abounding in love.... For as high as the heavens are above the earth, so great is his love for those who fear him;...

As a father has compassion on his children, so the LORD has compassion on those who fear him.

♥ Psalm 118:1, NIV
Give thanks to the LORD, for he is good; his love endures forever.

♥ Zephaniah 3:17, NIV
The LORD your God is with you, he is mighty to save. He will take great delight in you, he will quiet you with his love, he will rejoice over you with singing.

♥ John 3:16, 17, NIV
For God so loved the world that he gave his one and only Son, that whoever believes in him shall not perish but have eternal life. For God did not send his Son into the world to condemn the world, but to save the world through him.

♥ Romans 8:37-39, NIV
No, in all these things we are more than conquerors through him who loved us. For I am convinced that neither death nor life, neither angels nor demons, neither the present nor the future, nor any powers, neither height nor depth, nor anything else in all creation, will be able to separate us from the love of God that is in Christ Jesus our Lord.

♥ Ephesians 3:16-21, NIV
I pray that out of his glorious riches he may strengthen you with power through his Spirit in your inner being, so that Christ may dwell in your hearts through faith. And I pray that you, being rooted and established in love, may have power, together with all the saints, to grasp how wide and long and high and deep is the love of Christ, and to know this love that surpasses knowledge—that you may be filled to the measure of all the fullness of God. Now to him who is able to do immeasurably more than all we ask or imagine, according to his power that is at work within us, to him be glory in the church and in Christ Jesus throughout all generations, forever and ever! Amen.

♥ I John 4:9-10, NIV
This is how God showed his love among us: He sent his one and only Son into the world that we might live through him. This is love: not that we loved God, but that he loved us and sent his Son as an atoning sacrifice for our sins.

Which verse most reveals God's love to you?

_____

_____

_____

_____

_____

_____

Talk Points

♥ Read all of Psalm 103. Discuss the ways the psalmist, David, describes God. How do each of these characteristics and behaviors reveal His love?

_____

_____

_____

_____

♥ God did not bring instant healing to Tyler, but He revealed His love in the midst of pain. Read Hebrews 12:5-11. Everyone encounters difficulties, some a result of wrong choices and others a result of natural circumstances. But no matter the source of the difficulty, our response is formative. According to this passage, we can face difficulty with trust, understanding that God wants to build our character and teach us to rely on Him. How can God demonstrate His love in the midst of difficulty? How should we respond when we face trouble?

_____

_____

_____

_____

_____

_____

♥ We know that God is our Creator and that He reveals His love as He forgives, heals, restores, satisfies us with good things, is slow to anger, works for our good, shows compassion, and supplies our every need. Describe the depth of the relationship with Him that is available to us.

_____

_____

_____

_____

_____

_____

Journal Points

♥ God reveals His love for you in many different ways:
  • Through a loving family member—possibly a parent, grandparent, or aunt;
  • By giving you a new understanding of His character through His written word;

- By bringing you to a group of people who love Him and actively demonstrate His love to you;
- Through a specific encounter with a Christ-following individual;
- By stepping into your circumstances and providing what is needed.

James 1:17 tells us, "Every good and perfect gift is from above, coming down from the Father of heavenly lights, who does not change." What are the different ways God reveals His love for you?

_____

_____

_____

_____

_____

_____

_____

♥ Honestly ask yourself if something is hindering you from experiencing God's love. Psalm 62:8 invites us to, "Trust in him at all times, O people; pour out your hearts to him, for God is our refuge." He wants you to be honest with Him. Take some time to tell Him exactly how you feel; expect Him to respond.

_____

_____

_____

_____

_____

_____

_____

♥ Take some time to write out the characteristics of God (listed in Psalm 103 or other passages) and how each characteristic reveals His love for you.

_____

_____

_____

_____

Love ♥

Action Points

♥ If you need a fresh understanding of God's love, commit to setting time aside every day this week to read through the Scriptures listed in this lesson. Spend time talking to Him, and ask Him to reveal His love in a special way to you. Then consciously watch for His activity in your life. Read Jeremiah 29:11-13, and consider the directives and promises in this passage. Expect Him to respond.

_____

_____

_____

_____

_____

♥ Understanding that God often reveals His love through His followers, who could you show His love to this week? How will you do that?

_____

_____

_____

_____

_____

_____

_____

_____

Prayer Points

♥ Thank God for the many ways He has revealed His love to you.

♥ Ask God to reveal His love for you in a fresh, new way.

♥ Pray for those you love to experience a revelation of His love.

Consider the verses you've read. Then write out a prayer.

_____

_____

_____

_____

_____

_____

_____

_____

authentic love

Jodi Detrick

"Above all, love each other deeply"
(I Peter 4:8, NIV)

It may have sounded awkward to other people's ears, but it was as sweet as a bird's song after a thunderstorm to mine. "Bah-buh Jodi! Bah-buh Jodi!" The childish cry of delight came from a distance, across the crowded church foyer. I knew what would happen next. The one who had called out to me, a darling eight-year-old girl with a severe hearing impairment, would come running my way, face lit up. I would drop to my knee, and we would savor a big hug and a quick chat. Her mom would interpret with sign language when she couldn't quite lip-read what I was saying. I would try signing a few words I had learned that week in the sign-language class I was taking. Another hug and she would be on her way.

Bah-buh Jodi. Bible Jodi. None of us ever quite figured out how she came to call me by that name. Her mom had only started coming to our church at the invitation of a friend who told her we offered interpretation for the deaf in our services. With no previous church history, little Kacee didn't know I was the pastor's wife or what all that meant. She wasn't impressed with my knowledge of Scripture or my ability to teach it to others. All she knew is that, week after week, the lady with the Bible got down on one knee, gave her a big hug, and tried to make conversation with her. That's all.

Bah-buh Jodi. No matter what formal roles I fulfill or degrees I earn that may confer upon me a particular title, I think I will always be most humbled by that one and love it best. Being called "Bible Jodi" also gives me a pretty high standard to live up to, considering how "un-Bible Jodi-ish" I am at times!

To say the Bible is a complex book is probably the understatement of the... well, eternity ("century" is not quite long enough)! But if you had to boil it all down to a central theme, love keeps rising to the top. I think that's what Jesus was saying in Luke 10:27 (NIV): "He answered, 'Love the Lord your God with all your heart and with all your soul and with all your strength and with all your mind'; and, 'Love your neighbor as yourself.'"

In Matthew 7:12, Jesus explained that simply treating others the way you want to be treated is a good way to sum up everything the law and the prophets were trying to say. And 1 John 4:16 says, "God is love." It doesn't get much more "bottom line" than that.

We, who have had our hearts healed, our lives put back together, and our eternities redeemed by God's breathtaking love for us, know something in the deepest parts of us. We know we are loved, so we will love. There is an internal throbbing of God's heart for others, put there by His Spirit when He came to live in us, reminding us constantly that from now on, whatever else we are about while we live on the planet, loving is our real job. In fact, I Peter 4:8 (NIV) puts it like this: "Above all, love each other deeply." Above all...love deeply.

I wish I could say that loving is always a dream job, a piece of cupcake (with real buttercream frosting on top—I'm giving away one of my weaknesses!). It's not. Being nice to people you will never see again, and who manage not to bug you in the brief moments of an encounter, is not that tough. However, being nice when it's no bother, and loving authentically when it is, are two entirely different matters.

Here's the thing: real love connects. Always has, always will. God, Himself, set that precedent. Can you begin to imagine what our world would be like today if God had remained distant and disconnected from us in our need? We would not only be utterly broken but completely hopeless as well. You can be nice, yet aloof. But you cannot love and remain aloof. Real love connects.

In order to connect, though, barriers must be overcome, walls have to be scaled. And scaling walls of human resistance is hard, soul-breaking work... just ask Jesus. When I think of the most common barrier that keeps us from connecting in a way that produces authentic love, one major thing comes to mind: differentness.

"Differentness"

I'll never forget the first time I met a coworker named Sandy.* Long hair parted down the middle, no make-up, big plaid flannel shirt, almost worn-out Birkenstocks, and nursing her newborn...she looked like she would find a 1960s commune a little better fit than this medical office where I'd just been hired. When it came to professional settings, I was used to people dressing, acting, and speaking in certain ways.

Oh, she spoke in "certain ways," all right! It was soon pretty obvious that Sandy had a hair-trigger temper and quite a colorful vocabulary to go along with it. In addition to these other things, she and I couldn't have had a more different belief system. I was a church girl, a PK (preacher's kid), who was born and raised into a family of Christian believers. Sandy, too, was on a spiritual quest, but her searching had led her deeply into a blend of mysticism, eastern religions, and the New Age movement.

I remember her telling me about the "past existence work-ups" she'd been doing...working with a psychic to find out who she had been in previous lives. Knowing that, she explained, would help her figure out why she was having so many struggles dealing with this life. Maybe she could find some way to fix those problems, adjust her karma, and then things would be different.

Different? Sandy was so different—and we had to work together closely! *God, what in the world am I doing in this office?* I wondered. Yet the heart of Jesus, beating in me by His indwelling presence, compelled me to scale that wall of differentness. What I saw was the fear, confusion, and pain of a spiritually-hungry soul on the other side.

As our friendship progressed, I soon came to realize there was more to her as we invited Sandy and her husband over for dinner. Big-hearted, brilliant-

* Name and a few details changed to protect privacy.

minded, and fun—I grew to truly love this unique person. I was shocked when she quickly accepted my invitation to come to a women's event at our church—and moved as she quietly cried all the way through the speaker's message.

Through the months ahead, Sandy and I engaged in long, meaningful conversations about life and faith. What made Jesus any different than Buddha or Mohammed, she wanted to know. Why couldn't she just add Him to the rest of her "spiritual bag of tricks"? Time went by and our friendship continued to grow, despite our many differences. So did Sandy's spiritual hunger. I remember one phone call in particular. "Why can't I stop thinking about Jesus?" she wanted to know. "I'm even having dreams about Him. What's with that?"

You may have guessed the ending to God's loving pursuit of Sandy. I'll never forget the day when she approached me with a new expression on her face—one of hopefulness, light-heartedness, honest joy.

"Jodi!" she exclaimed. "You'll never guess!" (I already had.)

"Last night I went out into the field beside our house and knelt down in the grass. Something just broke open inside me, and I spent two hours pouring my heart out to God, asking His forgiveness for all the wrong I've done in my life, and inviting Jesus to live in me. I believe in Him, Jodi! I feel like I'm a whole new person!"

This may sound like the contrived script from some "cheesy Christian movie," but I assure you, it's not. That's exactly what happened, and Sandy was right. She was a whole new person, and her life completely changed in more ways than I have space to describe here. It was my privilege to spend time discipling Sandy and watching her grow as a believer. I have yet to see a more earnest or eager follower of Jesus. She devoured the Word of God and fought hard to change old, ingrained, destructive ways of thinking and acting. After a while, her husband and sons also became Christ-followers.

I loved the years of friendship our families shared, making the effort to get together now and then, even after we moved from the area. We had connected on a heart-level and "loved each other deeply," as I Peter 4:8 says to do.

That's why I wasn't surprised to get a long-distance call from Sandy on that early summer day more than a decade ago. We checked in with each other from time to time, and I was eager to hear the latest about her life and her family. Today, however, her voice had none of that feisty, exuberant tone I'd grown to love. "Jodi," she said quietly. "I've been to see the doctor, and they've been running some tests. I just got the results back today...it doesn't look good."

Climbing into my car to make the long drive to go and be with Sandy, I had plenty of time to pray. I knew God had the power to heal her and I pleaded for that. Later that day, we walked side by side down the long, country lane near her home. She processed her feelings aloud and expressed how much she wanted to be around to see her boys grow up. Later, through months of hospitalization, chemo, stem-cell transplants, and bone marrow transplants, we stayed connected. We would even "e-pray" back and forth together when her precarious condition prevented visitors.

Her faith never faltered, even when it was obvious the medical treatments were not working. She was allowed to go home for her final days on earth. Sandy's husband called one day and said she did not have long. My husband, Don, and I drove over to see her one more time. When we arrived at their home, we were told that she had slipped into a coma and was unresponsive.

As I knelt beside her bed, I took her hand and said, "Sandy, it has been one of the greatest privileges of my life to introduce you to Jesus. I never dreamed you would meet Him face to face before I do, though. So maybe when I get to heaven, you can take my hand and say, 'Jesus, this is Jodi!', okay?"

Sandy's eyes fluttered and she said the last word she would ever speak on earth. "Goodnight!"

"Goodnight, Sandy," I whispered. "I'll see you in the morning—in the eternal morning we'll share together someday."

Connection. It helps, even when it hurts...and it changes everything. Without it, there is no authentic love. It allows us to scale walls of differentness and see into the souls of others who make us uncomfortable with their words and actions. It is what caused the man we now call the "Good Samaritan" to cross the street and care for someone so different from himself (Luke 10:25-37). It is what sent Peter to share the good news with Cornelius (Acts 10:1-48), who had three strikes of differentness against him: he was a Roman (part of the hated oppressors), a centurion (a high-ranking soldier known for wielding cruel authority), and a Gentile (despised by religious Jews).

Authentic love that demands connection is what moved Jesus to defend a weeping, foot-washing prostitute (Luke 7:36-50). It is what enabled Him to spend three precious years of His short earthly life investing in a motley band of common fishermen. It is what caused Him to come after you and me, despite the many barriers our sinfulness has created…even when it meant the Cross.

Connection still matters if we are going to do our most important job as Christ-followers—loving others. Which reminds me…that little girl I told you about earlier? Kacee is all grown up and has graduated from high school. We moved away but a friend told me recently about the many medals she's won in the Special Olympics.

All I know is that, despite our differentness—and the fact that we had to work a little extra to scale a communication barrier—Kacee won my heart years ago with her warm smiles and big hugs. And perhaps in some small way, it was this little, but powerful, connection of authentic love on one knee that earned me the name "Bible Jodi."

Scripture Points

Consider how the following verses show authentic love connecting despite differences:

♥ Genesis 33:1-4, NIV
Jacob looked up and there was Esau, coming with his four hundred men; so he divided the children among Leah, Rachel and the two maidservants. He put the maidservants and their children in front, Leah and her children next, and Rachel and Joseph in the rear. He himself went on ahead and bowed down to the ground seven times as he

approached his brother. But Esau ran to meet Jacob and embraced him; he threw his arms around his neck and kissed him. And they wept.

♥ Ruth 1:16-18, NIV

But Ruth replied, "Don't urge me to leave you or to turn back from you. Where you go I will go, and where you stay I will stay. Your people will be my people and your God my God. Where you die I will die, and there I will be buried. May the LORD deal with me, be it ever so severely, if anything but death separates you and me." When Naomi realized that Ruth was determined to go with her, she stopped urging her.

♥ 1 Samuel 18:1-4, NIV

After David had finished talking with Saul, Jonathan became one in spirit with David, and he loved him as himself. From that day Saul kept David with him and did not let him return to his father's house. And Jonathan made a covenant with David because he loved him as himself. Jonathan took off the robe he was wearing and gave it to David, along with his tunic, and even his sword, his bow and his belt.

♥ 2 Samuel 9:6-7, NIV

When Mephibosheth son of Jonathan, the son of Saul, came to David, he bowed down to pay him honor.
David said, "Mephibosheth!"
"Your servant," he replied.
"Don't be afraid," David said to him, "for I will surely show you kindness for the sake of your father Jonathan. I will restore to you all the land that belonged to your grandfather Saul, and you will always eat at my table."

♥ 2 Kings 5:1-4, THE MESSAGE

Naaman was general of the army under the king of Aram. He was important to his master, who held him in the highest esteem because it was by him that GOD had given victory to Aram: a truly great man, but afflicted with a grievous skin disease. It so happened that Aram, on one of its raiding expeditions against Israel, captured a young girl who became a maid to Naaman's wife. One day she said to her mistress, "Oh, if only my master could meet the prophet of Samaria, he would be healed of his skin disease." Naaman went straight to his master and reported what the girl from Israel had said.

♥ Hosea 3:1-3, NIV
The LORD said to me, "Go, show your love to your wife again, though she is loved by another and is an adulteress. Love her as the LORD loves the Israelites, though they turn to other gods and love the sacred raisin cakes."

So I bought her for fifteen shekels of silver and about a homer and a lethek of barley. Then I told her, "You are to live with me many days; you must not be a prostitute or be intimate with any man, and I will live with you."

♥ Matthew 9:9-13, NIV
As Jesus went on from there, he saw a man named Matthew sitting at the tax collector's booth. "Follow me," he told him, and Matthew got up and followed him. While Jesus was having dinner at Matthew's house, many tax collectors and "sinners" came and ate with him and his disciples. When the Pharisees saw this, they asked his disciples, "Why does your teacher eat with tax collectors and 'sinners'?" On hearing this, Jesus said, "It is not the healthy who need a doctor, but the sick. But go and learn what this means: 'I desire mercy, not sacrifice.' For I have not come to call the righteous, but sinners."

♥ Matthew 19:4-6, NIV
"Haven't you read," he replied, "that at the beginning the Creator 'made them male and female,' and said, 'For this reason a man will leave his father and mother and be united to his wife, and the two will become one flesh'? So they are no longer two, but one. Therefore what God has joined together, let man not separate."

♥ Acts 9:15-19, NIV
But the Lord said to Ananias, "Go! This man is my chosen instrument to carry my name before the Gentiles and their kings and before the people of Israel. I will show him how much he must suffer for my name." Then Ananias went to the house and entered it. Placing his hands on Saul, he said, "Brother Saul, the Lord—Jesus, who appeared to you on the road as you were coming here—has sent me so that you may see again and be filled with the Holy Spirit." Immediately, something like scales fell from Saul's eyes, and he could see again. He got up and was baptized, and after taking some food, he regained his strength.

Which verse most reminds you of a difference you've seen overcome by authentic love?

_____

_____

Talk Points

♥ The verse at the start of this chapter, I Peter 4:8, says, "Above all, love each other deeply." But the rest of that verse says, "because love covers over a multitude of sins." What might it look like in the real world to "cover someone's sin" with love?

♥ Read verses 8-11 in that same chapter (I Peter 4). How do the things mentioned there help us make connections with others? What are the obstacles that women today must overcome to put those things into practice?

_____

_____

_____

_____

_____

_____

_____

_____

_____

_____

♥   In this chapter, you read about the connection Jodi made with Kacee and with Sandy. What were the things she had in common with each of them? Both were also different from her in unique ways. What were some of those differences? Are there some kinds of "differentness" that are easier to overcome than others? How can authentic love help us to connect despite the various types of differences we encounter?

_____

_____

_____

_____

_____

Journal Points

♥ Describe a time when it was hard for you to connect with someone who was very different than you. Were you able to overcome those differences and connect? If so, how? If not, how could you be prepared to do so next time?

_____

_____

_____

_____

_____

_____

♥ Take a few moments to consider all the walls God's authentic love had to scale to reach you. List some of those walls and also some of the ways that God would consider you "so different" from Him.

_____

_____

_____

_____

_____

_____

_____

♥ Think about someone who went over some kind of "wall of differentness" to connect with you. Write about how that experience made you feel and one way that you could forward that kindness on to someone else.

_____

_____

_____

_____

_____

_____

Action Points

♥ Write "Loving is my real job" on a sticky note and put it someplace where you will see it each day for the next week. At the end of the week, set aside ten minutes to write a possible "job description" of what authentic love would require in your life for the coming month. Be as specific as possible.

_____

_____

_____

_____

_____

_____

_____

_____

_____

_____

_____

_____

♥ Be on the alert for those whose differences might normally cause you to avoid them. Prayerfully ask for God's help and authentic love to scale those walls and make connection. Act when He gives you an opportunity, no matter how small.

_____

_____

_____

_____

_____

_____

_____

Prayer Points

♥ Each day in the week ahead, thank God for His love for you that connected, despite your many differences. For example: "God, You are so strong, and I am so weak" or "Father, you are so wise, and I am often foolish...thank you for loving me even though I am, by nature, so unlike You." Let this prayer focus renew your gratitude for His authentic love for you and spur you on to love others despite their differences.

♥ Choose one person who is very different from you (perhaps even in ways that make you uncomfortable) to pray for during the week ahead. Ask God for insights about how to pray for her or him most effectively and also for new ways to connect.

♥ If you find yourself in a comfort zone where practically all the people you interact with regularly are very similar to you in belief and lifestyle, ask God to help you have the courage to go outside that "safe sameness" and connect with others in your community who need to see the authentic love of God active in a real person.

Considering that real love connects despite differences, write out a short prayer asking God to let that be true in your life.

_____

_____

_____

_____

_____

_____

CHAPTER 3

transforming love

Joanna Weaver

"And my prayer is this: that your
love will abound more and more
in knowledge and depth of insight"
(Philippians 1:9, NIV)

I don't remember the moment I asked Jesus into my heart. I don't remember if it was in Sunday school or during bedtime prayers. When I've asked my parents, they can't pinpoint a time either. To be honest, that's always bothered me a little. When it comes time to give a testimony, it feels a little wishy-washy and drained of power when you can't remember a clear before-and-after conversion—a this-is-where-Jesus-changed-me moment to point to as evidence of salvation.

My spiritual journey has been more gradual than that. A slow change from the inside out. And yet, it has been as life-altering as any drug addict-turned-evangelist testimony I used to envy as a young Christian. Because, you see, even good girls need a Savior. Even after they're saved.

I was never an especially attractive child. Falling on the scale between plain and somewhat pretty, I was tall for my age and skinny, with stringy brown hair. But the worst defect, at least in my opinion, was my teeth. When one of my baby teeth fell out, a double tooth grew in to replace it. My dentist tried to reassure me that it was proof I was evolutionarily advanced beyond my peers—an explanation I never quite understood. All I knew is what I saw in the mirror. My smile looked weird. And looking weird, as all grade-schoolers know, is to be avoided at all costs.

So when I laughed I covered my mouth with my hand. When I smiled, I did it closed-mouthed or with my lip stretched over my top teeth in a strangled kind of grimace. In elementary pictures, my eyes look tentative as though I hope I don't look as bad as I'm certain I do.

Insecurity followed me into childhood friendships as well. So desperate for people to like me, no matter how hard I tried, I never fit in. I cringe to think of the silly things I did in my attempts to be accepted. It isn't surprising that my desperation was met with rejection. Junior high was incredibly painful. Looking back, however, I've learned to be grateful. That time brought me to the end of myself and helped me find the transforming love I so desperately needed.

The summer following my eighth-grade year, the one friendship I valued most was irretrievably lost and broken. I remember pouring out my pain at a summer camp altar, feeling as though my life were over. It was fertile ground for God to work.

For months, the Holy Spirit had been stirring my heart to all-out surrender—to go beyond knowing Jesus as my Savior and truly making Him my Lord. But fear was causing me to hold back.

The thought of such abandonment was terrifying. After all, who knew what God might ask if I gave up the right to myself and my plans and fully surrendered to His. What if God called me to be a missionary in Africa? What if He made me marry a short, balding man with acne on his forehead and forced me to live among pygmies for the rest of my life? It seemed quite dangerous to me, this idea of total surrender.

When I brought what I considered very legitimate concerns to God that night at the altar, He remained disturbingly quiet. Rather than whispering comfort and consolation, He just reiterated His claim on my life. "Jump, Joanna," I sensed the Father say as I stood, metaphorically speaking, on the edge of the black abyss of abandonment. There was no promise of safe passage. No clear landing site in view.

"You say you belong to me," the Lord whispered. "Prove it."

With the fine-feathered comfort of friendship and acceptance removed from the nest, I was finally ready to take the leap. "I'm scared, Lord, and I don't completely understand what this means," I prayed through tears, "but I'm Yours. You can have me completely. Come take the throne of my heart. Be the Lord of my life."

There at the altar, I felt something shift, as though a tug-of-war had finally been finished and a clear winner declared. A battle had been won, and somehow I knew it. Although there would be other skirmishes, other choices that would have to be made over the years to come, an important spiritual stalemate had been broken. Jesus was finally more than my Savior. He was now my Master, my Ruler, my Lord.

Something divine happened that night, but it wasn't until the next day that I fully realized a transformation had taken place. "What are you so happy about?" my roommates kept asking me, but I couldn't quite find the words to explain—until that night at the camp service when a chance comment helped me realize how much had changed.

"You really have a beautiful smile," a boy whispered behind me as we stood up to sing. *A beautiful smile?* I'd never heard those words before. But then I realized I'd been smiling the whole day. Really, truly smiling. Downright beaming, in fact.

Rather than covering my grin at his comment like I would have done before, the boy's kind words made me smile all the more. Not because a member of the opposite sex had noticed me (though that was nice) but because a stronghold had truly been broken.

From that moment on, I can honestly say that the debilitating self-consciousness concerning my smile disappeared. That's not to say I don't wish it was different some times. After all, my hair still tends to be straight and stringy and I'll always be stuck somewhere between plain and pretty, but I can assure you of this: I've been transformed. And you can be changed as well.

But it doesn't come through other people's approval or living life our own way. It comes through surrender, through complete abandonment to a love that we will never fully understand nor adequately deserve, through the absurd, yet courageous act of leaping into the great unknown called faith. And there we find the gracious arms of God awaiting us.

"Those who look to him are radiant," David writes in Psalm 34:5, "their faces are never covered with shame." That's the power of transforming love.

Scripture Points

God longs to transform our lives. What do the following verses suggest we do in order to cooperate with this work of grace in our lives?

♥ Romans 12:1-2, NIV
Therefore, I urge you, brothers and sisters, in view of God's mercy, to offer your bodies as a living sacrifice, holy and pleasing to God—this is your true and proper worship. Do not conform to the pattern of this world, but be transformed by the renewing of your mind. Then you will be able to test and approve what God's will is—his good, pleasing and perfect will.

♥ Philippians 2:12-13, NIV
Therefore, my dear friends, as you have always obeyed—not only in my presence, but now much more in my absence—continue to work out your salvation with fear and trembling, for it is God who works in you to will and to act in order to fulfill his good purpose.

♥ 2 Corinthians 5:17, NLT
This means that anyone who belongs to Christ has become a new person. The old life is gone; a new life has begun!

♥ Colossians 1:22-23, NIV
But now he has reconciled you by Christ's physical body through death to present you holy in his sight, without blemish and free from accusation—if you continue in your faith, established and firm, and do not move from the hope held out in the gospel. This is the gospel that you heard and that has been proclaimed to every creature under heaven, and of which I, Paul, have become a servant.

♥ 2 Peter 1:4, NIV
Through these he has given us his very great and precious promises, so that through them you may participate in the divine nature, having escaped the corruption in the world caused by evil desires.

♥ Ephesians 4:22-24, NIV
You were taught, with regard to your former way of life, to put off your old self, which is being corrupted by its deceitful desires; to be made new in the attitude of your minds; and to put on the new self, created to be like God in true righteousness and holiness.

♥ Ezekiel 36:26, NLT
And I will give you a new heart, and I will put a new spirit in you. I will take out your stony, stubborn heart and give you a tender, responsive heart.

♥ 1 Timothy 6:11, NIV
But you, man of God, flee from all this, and pursue righteousness, godliness, faith, love, endurance and gentleness.

♥ Philippians 1:9-11, NLT
I pray that your love will overflow more and more, and that you will keep on growing in knowledge and understanding. For I want you to understand what really matters, so that you may live pure and blameless lives until the day of Christ's return. May you always be filled with the fruit of your salvation—the righteous character produced in your life by Jesus Christ—for this will bring much glory and praise to God.

♥ Philippians 1:6, NIV
Being confident of this, that he who began a good work in you will carry it on to completion until the day of Christ Jesus.

Which verse speaks most to you concerning transformation?

_____

_____

_____

_____

Talk Points

♥ According to Romans 8:29, God's highest purpose is to make us like His Son. When you think of Jesus, which of His characteristics do you want (or need) most in your life? Be specific.

_____

_____

_____

_____

♥ Consider the following people from the Bible. How did God's love meet each of these women and transform their lives?

Woman at the well (John 4:13-15 and 28-30)

_____

_____

_____

_____

_____

_____

_____

Mary Magdalene (Luke 8:1-3)

_____

_____

_____

_____

_____

_____

Martha (Luke 10:40-42 and John 11:20-22)

_____

_____

_____

_____

_____

_____

_____

_____

_____

_____

♥ Colossians 3:8-14 tells us how we go about partnering with God in transformation. List the things we're told to "rid yourselves of" and the things to "clothe yourselves with"—what specific things on these lists do you need to work on?

GET RID OF:

_____

_____

_____

_____

_____

CLOTHE WITH:

_____

_____

_____

_____

_____

_____

Journal Points

♥ Draw a timeline of your life. Mark significant spiritual moments when you experienced God's transforming love—the warm-fuzzy times as well as the painful, hard times.

♥ Describe how those moments changed you.

_____

_____

_____

_____

_____

_____

_____

What area of your life do you feel God currently putting His finger on? Remember, He only reveals so He can heal. Write out a prayer giving God access to the place(s) that need His transforming love.

_____

_____

_____

_____

Action Points

Read Titus 2:11-12. True, lasting transformation requires our cooperation with grace. Using the scriptural outline below, list one practical way you could live out each category with the Holy Spirit's help.

Say "no" to ungodliness:_____

_____

_____

_____

Say "no" to worldly passions: _____

_____

_____

_____

_____

Live self-controlled: _____

_____

_____

_____

_____

Live upright and holy: _____

_____

_____

_____

♥ What hindrances to true transformation do you experience in "this present age"—the world and circumstances in which you live? What part does Jesus play in this process of changing us according to Titus 2:12?

_____

_____

_____

_____

_____

_____

_____

Prayer Points

♥   Thank God for His love and transforming power.

♥   Ask God to reveal anything He would like to change in you.

♥   Repent of any actions or attitudes you know are wrong. Be specific.

♥   Pray for the wisdom and power to cooperate with His work.

Consider the verses you've read, then write out a prayer.

_____

_____

_____

_____

_____

_____

_____

_____

_____

CHAPTER 4

love in motion

Janelle Hail

"Serve one another humbly in love"
(Galatians 5:13, NIV)

I caught a glimpse of the scar that traversed my young body where my breast used to be and longed to go back to a time when breast cancer had not invaded my life. I had avoided looking in the mirror for several days after surgery because I didn't want to face the fact that I had lost the loveliest part of my body.

Along with breast cancer came a sadness, as though I had lost a dear friend. Since I could not look at my own body without crying, how could I expect any other person to accept my disfigurement? I was left with not only a broken body but also a broken heart.

At the age of 34, I had breast cancer. With no history of breast cancer in my family, I had led a healthy lifestyle filled with exercise and good eating habits. Nothing about having breast cancer made sense. A week after surgery, I not only would have to confront my reflection in the mirror but the emotional turmoil that had torn my heart into shreds.

Facing My Fears

As I dressed one morning, I lingered in front of the mirror and looked at my body with pity and remorse. Then I thought, *I can't go through my life feeling sorry for myself or loathing my body, or I will be a miserable human being.*

I hung my head and softly cried in despair, saying aloud, "God, help me see myself as you see me." That's all I said, but it came from the depth of my being.

At the moment the words left my mouth, peace settled over me like a soft cloud and swept from the top of my head all the way down to my feet. It was as though a gentle rain had fallen on a parched wasteland. What I experienced was God's presence in my life during a great moment of need.

Unexpected Answer to Prayer

A flood of gratitude swirled around my body. I looked down at my feet and said aloud, "I have two feet that can take me where I need to go."

I looked at my hands as I held them in front of me and said, "I have two hands that can work."

I spoke out, "I have a mouth to speak and a heart to care."

Then I said, "Thank you, God. I see myself as you see me, a beautiful child, perfect and complete in your eyes."

That was the beginning of my journey away from devastation into the joy of living, but my walk with the Lord began years before.

Walk Where He Leads

I have served the Lord since I was nine years old. I surrendered my life to Jesus at the church prayer altar and never looked back to long for sin, despite the contrast of light and darkness in my life. Through the years, my precious, godly mother took my brother and me to church, while my father stood at the door, waving his fist and cursing us. Mother was a kind-hearted woman who took care of her husband, children, and household and served

God whole-heartedly. My decision to follow Christ was easy, since she had lovingly shown us the ways of the Lord.

Throughout my walk with the Lord, life has thrown obstacles, tragedies, and hard decisions at my doorstep. I have never desired to follow any path except His, desiring only to go where He wants me to go. To understand this, let's look at what was happening at the time I encountered breast cancer.

A Hopeful Future

My husband, Neal, and I had been happily married 15 years and had three sons, ages 13, 10, and 3. Neal was traveling on weekends to oversee the construction of our dream home in another city. I didn't have time for the intrusion of breast cancer.

The bitterness, despair, and depression surrounding my cancer and surgery caused a giant ball of painful emotions to form, knocking a big, black hole through my heart. It wasn't until I started volunteering for other organizations that the hole began to heal.

At one volunteer job, I was troubled to learn that there were hundreds of thousands of women with no medical assistance to get mammograms.

Why should any woman ever have to make a choice between getting a mammogram and having food on the table for her children? I thought.

This great need spurred my husband and me to start the National Breast Cancer Foundation in 1991, eleven years after my breast cancer surgery. The foundation provides free mammograms and educational resources to help underserved women make informed decisions about their healthcare.

By focusing on other people instead of my own inadequacies and insecurities, the black hole filled in. One day, I was taking a relaxing walk by the ocean and realized the despair was gone. I hadn't even noticed when it left. My life and my destiny were changed forever.

As I dug past my emotional scars, God's love revealed a treasure trove of precious jewels. Where there was once turmoil, I found peace. Where there was once self-loathing, I found acceptance. Where there was once fear, I found hope. I stepped out of my dark despair into His light.

The Brightness of His Light

How bright is God's light as He mends and molds a broken vessel to pour out His love over hearts that are needy and destitute?

I remember the first few days after I came home from the hospital. We lived in West Texas where the wind blew against scrubby trees and aimlessly flung dirt down the street to the neighbors' yards. As I stood at the kitchen sink looking through a garden window while rinsing dishes from the evening meal, I spotted a lone four-foot tree in our yard. Autumn had come swiftly that year and carried away all the leaves except one fat, brilliant red leaf that hung on like a flag flapping in the breeze. It almost seemed to be happy as though it was riding on a roller coaster and squealing with joy. I laughed out loud, and thought, *What does that red leaf have to be happy about?* That was the moment I knew I wanted to be like that red leaf, brilliant to the end. I may not be brilliant yet, but I am hanging on for the joy of the work God has placed in my hands. To commemorate my epiphany at the kitchen sink, the image of a branch with leaves, indicating life, growth, and hope for a future became a part of the National Breast Cancer Foundation's logo. We have used it since its inception.

Where Will He Take Me?

In serving others, the Lord has led me day by day to reach into the lives of thousands of women who desperately need help across all 50 states and to provide them with medical services at their local hospitals. Now that the National Breast Cancer Foundation has gone international, we are able to reach across five continents with life-saving educational resources.

Following my mastectomy, the days I spent in the hospital were the darkest times of my life. I was afraid my husband would leave me, but he didn't. We will celebrate our 46th wedding anniversary in August 2011.

I was afraid that society would reject me, but it didn't. At a time when people who had cancer didn't talk about it publicly, I found that my openness and candor helped others who had the same issues.

I was afraid that my life was over, and all of my hopes for a happy future were dashed. Instead, the course of my life was redirected into a grand plan designed by my Heavenly Father.

I remember praying in my hospital room and dedicating my tragic circumstances to the Lord to use for His glory. I addressed cancer and said, "Cancer, you are my enemy. You have tried to take my life and destroy me. You have lurked in darkness and terrorized me. Now, I am going to go after you. I will hunt you down to shine a bright light on your evil deeds and expose you with knowledge so you can no longer harm women. I am now your enemy."

That declaration was infused with the strength of the Lord and gave me the courage to boldly seek ways to help educate women with life-saving information about the early detection of breast cancer. Today, the National Breast Cancer Foundation shines a bright light through our online global educational tool, *Beyond The Shock* (www.BeyondTheShock.com), to address the questions women have about breast cancer. Now, no woman will ever have to walk in darkness but can find hope for her future.

No Longer Alone

I am not defined by breast cancer but by the way I have lived my life every day since. As you work through this study, pray about what opportunities you may have to let the ordinary things in life, the upsets and misfortunes and the feelings of inadequacy, become stepping stones into your future. You are never alone with Jesus holding onto you. You will walk the right path because the light of His love brightens your pathway. Even if you stumble and fall, He will pick you up and give you a life to serve others. And, you can be sure, it will be better than anything you could ever imagine.

He incorporates all of your God-given talents, training, skills, relationships, and ideas into a lovely plan for your future. Live your life with full joy, for in Him you have an abundance of everything you will need in this lifetime!

Scripture Points

Consider how the following verses describe God's love in motion in your life:

♥ Psalm 147:3, NIV
He heals the brokenhearted and binds up their wounds.

♥ I John 4:18, NIV
There is no fear in love. But perfect love drives out fear, because fear has to do with punishment. The one who fears is not made perfect in love.

♥ Psalm 100:4, NIV
Enter his gates with thanksgiving and his courts with praise; give thanks to him and praise his name.

♥ I Thessalonians 5:18, NIV
Give thanks in all circumstances; for this is God's will for you in Christ Jesus.

♥ Luke 24:45, NIV
Then he opened their minds so they could understand the Scriptures.

♥ Psalm 25:12, NIV
Who, then, are those who fear the LORD? He will instruct them in the ways they should choose.

♥ I John 5:14, NIV
This is the confidence we have in approaching God: that if we ask anything according to his will, he hears us.

♥ Psalm 57:7, NLT
My heart is confident in you, O God; my heart is confident. No wonder I can sing your praises!

♥ Psalm 147:11, NIV
The LORD delights in those who fear him, who put their hope in his unfailing love.

♥ Romans 15:13, Amplified
May the God of your hope so fill you with all joy and peace in believing [through the experience of your faith] that by the power of the Holy Spirit you may abound and be overflowing (bubbling over) with hope.

Which verse helps you understand how to put love in motion as you serve others?

_____

_____

_____

_____

_____

_____

_____

_____

Talk Points

♥   What is one of the dearest moments in which you have experienced the presence of God?

_____

_____

_____

_____

_____

_____

♥ Read the "love chapter," I Corinthians 13, and discuss times you have exhibited godly characteristics in difficult times.

_____

_____

_____

_____

_____

_____

♥ Discuss what it means to fear the Lord.

_____

_____

_____

_____

_____

_____

_____

_____

_____

_____

Journal Points

♥ What are the fears that keep you from moving forward? Be honest with God, and then you can be honest with yourself and others.

_____

_____

_____

_____

_____

_____

♥ What are some characteristics that are opposite of your fears that you would like to see working in your life?

_____

_____

_____

_____

_____

_____

_____

♥ If you had no obstacles, what dreams would you like to see fulfilled in your life?

_____

_____

_____

_____

_____

_____

_____

Love

Action Points

♥ Now that you clearly understand what has hindered you in the past and where you want to go in the future, what steps will you take to move forward? Remember that baby steps lead to greater steps. Don't worry about how to get to the big things. That will come in a natural process of time. Keep your eyes on the Lord, and He will reveal His plan to you.

_____

_____

_____

_____

_____

_____

_____

_____

_____

_____

_____

♥ How can you serve others with your gifts? As I grew up, I remember countless times watching my mother tote the lid of a cardboard box filled with baked goods to the car to deliver to friends who were ill or needed help. At the age of 80, she was still taking the "old people" to appointments because they couldn't drive. Bloom where you are planted! Make your action steps precise, and you will be able to clearly focus on the most important things.

_____

_____

_____

_____

_____

_____

_____

_____

Prayer Points

♥ Acknowledge God's love every day, and prayerfully watch for His blessings.

♥ Ask God for His wisdom to walk down His pathway.

♥ Pray for those whose lives you touch.

♥ Ask God for opportunities to bless and serve others.

As God speaks to your heart about what you have studied, write out a prayer to pray over yourself each day:

_____

_____

_____

_____

_____

_____

_____

_____

_____

_____

_____

Chapter 5

extravagant love

JoAnn Butrin

"The only thing that counts is
faith expressing itself through love"
(Galatians 5:6, NIV)

She walked as though she were carrying the weight of the world on her shoulders. When I looked into her eyes, I saw such sadness and despair. I met Catherine in the African country of Zambia, where I was doing some missions work focused on HIV/AIDS. Catherine was the head of a small, indigenous organization, which raised money to purchase limited amounts of food for persons suffering from AIDS and related illnesses and who could not fend for themselves. All six staff members of this organization were HIV positive themselves, including Catherine.

We accompanied Catherine and her team on "home visits" to those who were very ill with AIDS, delivering small parcels of food. We asked if we could pray for those we encountered, some so sick they could barely respond. I noted that Catherine did not join in the prayer and stood back as we "laid our hands" on one after another.

Even though I was emotionally exhausted after a heart-wrenching day of seeing so much pain and suffering, I felt a nudging in my spirit to spend some alone time with Catherine. I said to her, "You look so sad, and I feel you are heavy-hearted. Is there something I can pray with you about?" Those sad eyes filled with tears, and she began to tell me her story: her husband, who had been unfaithful, had brought HIV home to her and then became ill with AIDS. She was pregnant at the time, but instead of leaving him, she tended him till his death. Not long after, tests showed she was HIV positive, as was her small child.

She decided to go back to her home village to share her story with her pastor and family. The pastor told her she could not attend church but must sit on the outside. Her family wanted nothing to do with her.

Rejected, stigmatized and alone, she returned to the city to figure out how to survive. But her heart had filled with bitterness and anger toward God and the church.

I know a little about stigma. My father, a divine healing evangelist, became mentally ill in his early 50s and took his own life. I felt so ashamed that this had occurred in our "Christian, ministry-oriented" family. For many years, I felt like I wore a big "S" for suicide on my chest. It was a "self-imposed" stigma, I found out later, but one that existed nonetheless. I suffered silently, refusing to speak of it to anyone for many years. Though I did not leave my faith, I also felt anger and bitterness against God.

My heart was so drawn to Catherine, perhaps somewhat from my own experience. I asked her how it was that she was serving others when she was angry with God and the church. She responded that she knew she would be that sick one day (this was before most people had access to drugs), and she hoped someone would help her. I asked how she felt about the Lord at the time. She began to weep and said these words, "I miss Him!" In those moments, we prayed together, and repeating after me, she asked Jesus to come back into her heart and to fill her with His love and peace.

Our local missionary in Zambia connected her with a church, which received her with open arms and provided a safe refuge for her. Today, Catherine continues to head the same organization, now based in the very same church which took her in. She and her child have been able to receive the antiretroviral (anti-aids medications), and her health has been restored. What fills me with joy is to hear how she now conducts her home visits—praying for each person and sharing Christ with those who don't know Him—demonstrating extravagant love to those in tremendous need.

Through no fault of her own, a woman was infected with a life-threatening virus, passing that on to her child. She was then stigmatized and rejected by all those who should have been embracing her with love and acceptance. Once she did find that love again, from the Heavenly Father and the body of believers who surrounded her, she was able to forgive and to let go of the anger and bitterness. She blossomed into a beautiful servant of Christ, "expressing her faith through love."

I was concerned when I heard that two psychologists plus a group of American women who had suffered various forms of abuse were heading to Bosnia to minister to women raped and horribly abused during their country's war. I wondered if the difference in culture would make it difficult to relate and if they could really be effective. The group had the foresight to discuss this potential problem with Bosnian church leaders and Bosnian women of faith, asking what was really needed and how the volunteers could work through the church.

The church said it would be good to have some of their lay leaders trained to minister to the women who had suffered so much, but they also felt that if the American women shared some of their experiences of abuse, it would impact the Bosnian women.

It was amazing, I'm told, what an impact the stories had on the Bosnian women who had suffered abuse, to hear that Western women could suffer similarly. The tears, embraces and quickly formed relationships between the two groups resulted in some of them receiving Christ and being assimilated into the body of believers. Pastors, lay leaders and others received training by the American group so they could continue ministry after the group left.

It was inconvenient for the group to go all that way. It certainly cost quite a bit financially. And it surely had emotional cost. Every time I share about the suicide in my family, I still hear my voice quiver and wonder if I should. Yet on almost every occasion, it seems to minister to someone. I'm sure when the abused women shared their stories, it dredged up wounds from the past that had to be dealt with again. Yet their extravagant love and willingness to serve brought healing, wholeness and the transforming love of the Father to many broken lives.

The world is full of hurting people, often trapped in circumstances beyond their control—poverty, sickness, hunger, homelessness, abuse, and broken relationships, often directly or indirectly a result of sin and evil. Many, like myself, suffer silently from past or inner hurts no one even knows about. I love the Scripture that says, "But where sin increased, grace increased all the more" (Romans 5:20b). And earlier in the same chapter, these words so resonate as the answer for the world's suffering:

> Therefore, since we have been justified through faith, we have peace with God through our Lord Jesus Christ, through whom we have gained access by faith into this grace in which we now stand. And we rejoice in the hope of the glory of God. Not only so, but we also rejoice in our sufferings, because we know that suffering produces perseverance; perseverance, character; and character, hope. And hope does not disappoint us, because God has poured out his love into our hearts by the Holy Spirit, whom he has given us. (Romans 5:1-5, NIV)

How can we, as women of God, be involved in the hardships and suffering that are present both near and far? Can we individually and corporately really make a difference in the lives of those who are spiritually lost and in pain? Can we, as the Scripture says, be a part of the instrument of grace and love extravagantly, pouring it out to others?

First, as I know and understand the love of God that was given for me—a love so profound that He gave his son to die, a love that caused blood to be shed for me—how can I not reach out in and through that love, extend it to others? "Mostly what God does is love you. Keep company with Him and learn a life of love. Observe how Christ loved us. His love was not cautious but extravagant. He didn't love in order to get something from us, but to give everything of Himself to us. Love like that" (Ephesians 5:1-2, THE MESSAGE).

Second, I would say that everyone has gone through pain in one form or another. From my own experience with a family suicide, the resulting stigma and what I felt would be rejection, I deeply identified with this young woman and her pain in Zambia. And I've been amazed at how finally breaking silence and sharing in select audiences about my situation, led not to rejection but to others with similar situations who needed to "let it out." Just by being willing to share and overcome the shame of what happened, I have been afforded many ministry opportunities. I realized the body of Christ was there offering love and acceptance and not the rejection I imagined would be found.

Isn't it amazing how God can take both the good and the negative experiences of our lives and weave them into a tapestry that can become a blanket of protection and a covering of love for not only ourselves, but for those to whom we minister? As extravagant love from the Father fills us to overflowing, we can pour out the oil of healing and blessing to the hurting around us.

Third, we are instructed to "go." Nothing I see in the Bible tells us to sit behind the walls of the church and wait for the hurting to come to us, but rather the Scripture takes us to the "near" (our Jerusalem) around us and those at the "ends of the earth" (Matthew 28:19). I'm sure God could have found another way to touch Catherine's heart and draw her to Himself, but amazingly He chose me to be His channel. I "went" in obedience to His instruction to "go," and a wonderful miracle occurred in a dear woman's life. Why me? Probably, it was also for me, because it was a profound privilege and blessing to be the one who was there for her.

I love the story of the Good Samaritan found in Luke 10, as it gives us a beautiful portrayal of extravagant love. It demonstrates a commitment to be interrupted, inconvenienced, and to not offer just immediate relief, but to follow up and make sure that all is well. It's a complete picture of ministering one to another and sacrificial service. And He tells us, "to do likewise."

When you and I are willing, the Lord can use us to make a difference in the lives of those who are hurting and in need – both near and far. We can proclaim the Good News and see lives transformed by His saving grace and filled to overflowing with His love so that those who receive His love might then become a channel of blessing to others.

"But for right now, until that completeness, we have three things to do to lead us toward that consummation: Trust steadily in God, hope unswervingly, love extravagantly. And the best of the three is love" (1 Corinthians 13:13, THE MESSAGE).

Scripture Points

♥ Galatians 5:6, THE MESSAGE
For in Christ, neither our most conscientious religion nor disregard of religion amounts to anything. What matters is something far more interior: faith expressed in love.

♥ James 1:27, ESV
Religion that is pure and undefiled before God, the Father, is this: to visit orphans and widows in their affliction, and to keep oneself unstained from the world.

♥ Proverbs 19:17, THE MESSAGE
Mercy to the needy is a loan to GOD, and GOD pays back those loans in full.

♥ I John 3:17,18, NIV
If anyone has material possessions and sees his brother in need but has no pity on him, how can the love of God be in him?

♥ Psalm 82:3, ESV
Give justice to the weak and the fatherless; maintain the right of the afflicted and the destitute.

♥ Proverbs 21:13, NIV
If a man shuts his ears to the cry of the poor, he too will cry out and not be answered.

♥ Proverbs 28:27, NIV
Those who give to the poor will lack nothing, but those who close their eyes to them receive many curses.

♥ Proverbs 22:9, NIV
The generous will themselves be blessed, for they share their food with the poor.

♥ I Corinthians 4:1-2, NIV
This, then, is how you ought to regard us: as servants of Christ and as those entrusted with the mysteries God has revealed.

♥ I Timothy 6:17-19, THE MESSAGE

Tell those rich in this world's wealth to quit being so full of themselves and so obsessed with money, which is here today and gone tomorrow. Tell them to go after God, who piles on all the riches we could ever manage—to do good, to be rich in helping others, to be extravagantly generous. If they do that, they'll build a treasury that will last, gaining life that is truly life.

Talk Points

♥ The Apostle Paul says the only thing that counts is faith expressing itself through love (Galatians 5:6). Can you think of a time when someone expressed his or her faith by reaching out to you in love? Describe what happened and how it made you feel.

_____

_____

_____

_____

_____

_____

_____

_____

_____

_____

♥ We all know people like Catherine, who are angry with God and/or the church. How do tangible acts demonstrate the love of Christ more effectively than words sometimes?

_____

_____

_____

_____

_____

_____

_____

♥ What do you think was the biggest contributing factor that enabled Catherine to let go of her anger and bitterness?

_____

_____

_____

_____

_____

_____

_____

_____

Journal Points

♥ JoAnn mentions the stigma she grew up with because her father committed suicide. How can you overcome your aversion to a specific uncomfortable situation that makes you want to avoid reaching out?

_____

_____

_____

_____

_____

_____

_____

_____

♥ God can use both the positive and negative in our lives for His good and His glory. What is something you have experienced in your life—where you watched God make beauty out of ashes—that you might be able to share with someone else who is hurting and in need of encouragement?

_____

_____

_____

_____

_____

_____

_____

_____

_____

_____

♥   In *The Message*, I Corinthians 13:13, it says, "Trust steadily in God, hope unswervingly, love extravagantly." What might it look like to "trust steadily"?

_____

_____

_____

_____

_____

_____

_____

_____

_____

_____

What might it look like to "hope unswervingly"?

_____

_____

_____

_____

_____

_____

What might it look like to "love extravagantly"?

_____

_____

_____

_____

_____

_____

Love

Action Points

♥ Read this verse again: "Mostly what God does is love you. Keep company with Him and learn a life of love. Observe how Christ loved us.
His love was not cautious but extravagant. He didn't love in order to
get something from us, but to give everything of Himself to us. Love
like that" (Ephesians 5:1-2, THE MESSAGE). Find someone to ob-

serve this week who is showing extravagant love to others. Take notes of specific ways this person shows extravagant love. Send that person a note, thanking her for being a model of Christ loving us.

_____

_____

_____

_____

_____

_____

_____

_____

♥ This week, listen for the Holy Spirit to nudge you toward someone you need to spend time with. Find someone who, like Catherine, has "sad eyes or a heavy heart." Like JoAnn, ask that person what you could pray specifically about with her.

_____

_____

_____

_____

_____

_____

_____

_____

_____

_____

_____

Love

Prayer Points

♥   Continue praying every day for one week or longer for the person you
found to pray with in Action Points.

♥   JoAnn wrote: "As extravagant love from the Father fills us to overflowing, we can pour out the oil of healing and blessing to the hurting
around us." Pray for the Father to show you ways that you can be one
who pours out "oil of healing and blessing" to those around you.

Write out your prayer here:

_____

_____

_____

_____

Chapter 6

consuming love

Kerry Clarensau

"Love the Lord your God with all
your heart and with all your soul
and with all your mind and with all
your strength" (Mark 12:30, NIV)

My husband, Mike, and I were driving through our neighborhood to a party, when his phone rang. It was my mom. My first thought was, *I wonder why she is calling him and not me?* I quickly checked to see if I had missed her call or if my phone was on the silent setting.

Only seconds into his conversation, I was distracted by the heaviness in his tone of voice. When Mike stopped driving and pulled our car to the side of the street, I knew something was wrong. He told me my dad had just collapsed with a cardiac arrest. He was receiving CPR, but his heart wasn't beating on its own. My mom thought he was gone.

But God positioned an experienced CPR instructor and a top-notch first response team to be with my dad at just the right moment. The EMTs shocked his heart several times before it began beating on its own, and then he was transported by helicopter to a wonderful cardiac hospital.

The doctors didn't know if my dad would ever regain consciousness, or if he did, how much damage was already done to his vital organs. But they decided to try a relatively new hypothermic treatment, which lowers body temperature and allows the organs to regain function slowly, preventing any further damage. (They literally put my dad on ice.)

My dad was in very critical condition for nine days. When someone we love is so near death, it is as if everything stops, and our entire world is engulfed in the four walls of the hospital. For the first couple of days we never left the building. We spent every minute sitting in the waiting room or huddled by dad's bed, watching machines sustain his life.

We felt like we were "walking through the valley of the shadow of death." In that valley, the most important things of life are in full view—our relationship with God and those He has given us to love. That is it; nothing else seems to matter.

We spent hours with our family and friends who lovingly surrounded us. In those unforgettable moments, we gain a priceless glimpse into the souls of those closest to us. I saw a strength in my mom I didn't know existed, a level of maturity in my young adult children which made my heart smile, a tenderness in my husband that helped soothe our pain, a love in my extended family that made me proud to be one of them, and practical acts of kindness from friends that comforted our tired bodies.

I must tell you, we experienced God's amazing love in so many ways! One of those precious moments came through an encounter with someone we'd never met before. And even now, we don't know his name.

Several days in a row, I observed the hospital janitor in the Intensive Care Unit. He carefully swept and mopped the floors of each room. But I noticed before he moved to the next area, he would pause for several moments, lean against the handle of his mop, and look tenderly at the patient. I couldn't help but wonder if he was praying.

Late one evening, after a day that seemed to stretch out like a week, the same janitor walked into the waiting room where we were "camping out." He apologized for interrupting and asked if he could sweep while we were in the room. We assured him that we didn't mind and quickly picked up our things from the floor.

Humming as he swept, he carried a noticeably calm presence into the room. My aunt asked if he liked to sing, and he said, "Oh, yes ma'am, I do!" He didn't seem rattled when she asked him to sing something for us. He just continued sweeping as a song poured effortlessly from his heart.

I don't remember all of his song, but the chorus went something like this: "I'm walkin' and talkin' with my mind set on Jesus…there's peace, there's joy, there's love as I keep on walkin' and talkin' with my Jesus…".

I have to tell you—tears were streaming down my cheeks as this precious man sang. His song explained the reason for his peaceful countenance. We were witnessing firsthand a man whose humble life was worship to the One he loved.

Before he left, I asked him if he was praying for the patients as he cleaned the Intensive Care Unit. And he responded, "Oh, yes ma'am. It is a privilege to pray for every one of them!" I wanted to run and hug him, but I didn't want to make a scene and embarrass my family. So I just quietly thanked him for praying for my dad.

I know the doctors and nurses played an important role in my dad's complete recovery. But I will never forget the prayers or the heart song of this sweet, anonymous janitor.

When I was about 27 years old, someone gave me a copy of the book, *The Practice of the Presence of God*. It describes the journey of Brother Lawrence, a Frenchman who served as a cook in a 17th century monastery. His desire was to live every moment with an overwhelming awareness of God's presence.

Consumed with love for God, Brother Lawrence wanted to perform every task, no matter how insignificant, purely for the love of God. His life has taught me what it looks like to actually live a life of worship, and not just participate in worship services. He was a living picture of one who loved God with all of his heart, soul, mind, and strength.

This may sound strange, but I consider Brother Lawrence to be a mentor. (Don't worry, I don't see or hear him! I've just learned so much from his writings.) His life challenges me to enjoy a closer relationship with God— one more intimate than I ever thought possible.

I'm sure I don't yet understand the depth of this reality—living continually aware of God's presence. But the little I have learned has completely transformed my life.

When I'm not living aware of God, my flesh wants to react and respond in ways that are anything but pleasing to Him. I easily become distracted, frustrated, fearful, and overwhelmed with the responsibilities and cares of life. And my words and behavior are always disappointing.

However, if I make every effort to "walk and talk" with God, my responses are completely different. When I am aware of Him, I can rely on Him for whatever I need in each moment—whether it is wisdom, insight, strength, love, or patience.

Brother Lawrence said it this way:

> We can do nothing without Him. But when we are faithful to keep ourselves in His holy presence, and set Him always before us, this not only hinders our offending Him and doing anything that may displease Him, at least willfully, but it also begets us in a holy freedom to ask successfully for the graces we stand in need of.[1]

I've often wondered if Brother Lawrence from the 17th century and Enoch from the Old Testament have something in common. Hebrews 11 tells us that Enoch was commended as one who pleased God, but all we know about him was that he walked with his Creator. Later in Hebrews 11:6, we are told that God rewards those who earnestly seek Him.

Both of these men teach us a very important lesson. Loving God is most evident as we simply walk with Him every moment and seek Him with all of our hearts.

It may seem like an overwhelming assignment, to be consciously aware of God's presence in our busy, distracted lives. But I have learned from Brother Lawrence—and the janitor—that you can have an ongoing "secret conversation of the soul" with God in the busiest moments.

Listen to what was said about this mentor of mine:

---

1   Brother Lawrence, *The Practice of the Presence of God* (Uhrichsville, OH: Barbour and Company, Inc., 1993,) 37-38.

As Brother Lawrence had found such an advantage in walking in the presence of God, it was natural for him to recommend it earnestly to others; but his example was a stronger inducement than any arguments he could propose. His very countenance was edifying, such a sweet and calm devotion appearing in it as could not but affect the beholders. And it was observed that in the greatest busyness in the kitchen he still preserved his recollection and heavenly mindedness. He was never hasty nor loitering, but did each thing in its season, with an even, uninterrupted composure and tranquility of spirit. "The time of busyness," said he, "does not with me differ from the time of prayer, and in the noise and chatter of my kitchen, while several persons are at the same time calling for different things, I possess God in as great tranquility as if I were upon my knees in prayer."[2]

The first time I read *The Practice of the Presence of God*, I was a young mother of two very active little boys. I discovered I could wipe runny noses, referee disputes, and make peanut butter sandwiches for the Lord. It completely changed how I approached my day—I wanted to do everything with excellence. And I grew to depend on Him more every day. It was so exciting to realize that He was right there to give me everything I needed to be a mom.

May Brother Lawrence challenge us to practice the presence of God! Or maybe the simple song of the janitor will become your own, "I'm walkin' and talkin' with my mind set on Jesus." Remember, there's peace, there's joy, there's love as we keep on walkin' and talkin' with our Jesus.

If you would like to join me on this life-long adventure of daily worship, join your heart with mine as we read Brother Lawrence's prayer:

> O my God, since Thou art with me, and I must now, in obedience to Thy commands, apply my mind to these outward things, I beseech Thee to grant me the grace to continue in Thy presence; and to this end do Thou prosper me with Thy assistance, receive all my works, and possess all my affections.[3]

That is true worship—may He possess all our affections!

---

2 Ibid., 34.
3 Ibid., 32-33.

Scripture Points

♥ Mark 12:30 , NIV
Love the Lord your God with all your heart and with all your soul and with all your mind and with all your strength.

♥ Hebrews 11:5-6, NIV
By faith Enoch was taken from this life, so that he did not experience death; he could not be found, because God had taken him away. For before he was taken, he was commended as one who pleased God. And without faith it is impossible to please God, because anyone who comes to him must believe that he exists and that he rewards those who earnestly seek him.

♥ Psalm 16:11, NIV
You make known to me the path of life; you will fill me with joy in your presence, with eternal pleasures at your right hand.

♥ Psalm 73:25-26, NIV
Whom have I in heaven but you? And earth has nothing I desire besides you. My flesh and my heart may fail, but God is the strength of my heart and my portion forever.

♥ Psalm 27:4, NIV
One thing I ask of the LORD, this is what I seek: that I may dwell in the house of the LORD all the days of my life, to gaze upon the beauty of the LORD and to seek him in his temple.

♥ Lamentations 3:22-23, NIV
Because of the LORD's great love we are not consumed, for his compassions never fail. They are new every morning; great is your faithfulness.

♥ Colossians 3:1-4, NIV
Since, then, you have been raised with Christ, set your hearts on things above, where Christ is seated at the right hand of God. Set your minds on things above, not on earthly things. For you died, and your life is now hidden with Christ in God. When Christ, who is your life, appears, then you also will appear with him in glory.

♥ Colossians 3:15-17, NIV
Let the peace of Christ rule in your hearts, since as members of one body you were called to peace. And be thankful. Let the word of Christ dwell in you richly as you teach and admonish one another with all wisdom, and as you sing psalms, hymns and spiritual songs with gratitude in your hearts to God. And whatever you do, whether in word or deed, do it all in the name of the Lord Jesus, giving thanks to God the Father through him.

♥ I Thessalonians 5:16-18, NIV
Rejoice always; pray continually; give thanks in all circumstances, for this is God's will for you in Christ Jesus.

♥ Hebrews 13:15, NIV
Through Jesus, therefore, let us continually offer to God a sacrifice of praise—the fruit of lips that confess his name.

Which of these scriptures most compels you to seek more of God and to dwell every moment in His presence?

_____

_____

_____

_____

_____

_____

_____

_____

Talk Points

♥ Imagine if Jesus walked into the room where you are sitting right now. How would you respond? How would His physical presence impact your behavior if He spent every moment of this day with you?

_____

_____

_____

_____

_____

_____

_____

♥ We know that God is always with us, but many times we live without giving much thought of His presence. What simple things can we do to continually remind ourselves that He is with us?

_____

_____

_____

_____

_____

_____

_____

♥ First Thessalonians 5:17 encourages us to pray continually. Brother Lawrence challenges his readers to abide in God's presence by continually conversing with Him. Describe the type of relationship we can have with God when we are in continual communication with Him.

_____

_____

_____

_____

_____

_____

♥ Read Colossians 3:17 and 3:23. Brother Lawrence was "resolved to make the love of God the end of all his actions. He was pleased when he could take up a straw from the ground for the love of God."[4] How can we turn our daily tasks into worship?

_____

_____

_____

_____

_____

_____

_____

4   Ibid., 15.

Journal Points

♥ Think about a time when you felt the overwhelming presence of God in prayer. Describe what it might be like to walk in the same awareness throughout your day.

_____

_____

_____

_____

_____

_____

_____

♥ Are there any activities, thought patterns, attitudes, or conversations in your life where you feel you must ignore God's presence in order to participate? How can you walk away from these destructive behaviors?

_____

_____

_____

_____

_____

_____

_____

_____

_____

♥ List the things in your life which create the greatest distractions from God's presence. How can you choose to live in His presence even in the busy moments of life?

_____

_____

_____

_____

_____

♥ Write a new commitment to be consumed with love for God—acknowledging His presence every moment. Include your desire for a renewed, ongoing "secret conversation of the soul." Knowing that your life can be worship, how would you describe your heart song?

_____

_____

_____

_____

_____

Action Points

♥ Write out the words, "Practice His Presence," on a 3x5 card or a sticky note. Put it where you will see it throughout the day. Let it remind you to consciously be aware of Him. Strive to keep an ongoing "secret conversation of the soul" with God. At the end of the day, record all of the ways your conversation impacted you.

_____

_____

_____

_____

_____

_____

_____

♥ Brother Lawrence said he wanted to do every task for the love of God. Think about everything you have to do today. How can you do every task for Him, creating a life of worship?

_____

_____

_____

_____

Prayer Points

♥ Acknowledge the challenge to abide in God's presence and ask for His help to be aware of Him throughout your day.

♥ Make a fresh commitment to the Lord to live a life of worship—doing everything for Him.

♥ Reread Brother Lawrence's prayer at the end of this chapter and make it your own.

Consider the verses you've read, then write out a prayer.

_____

_____

_____

_____

_____

_____

_____

epilogue
Kerry Clarensau

It doesn't matter if you are 18 years old or 85 years old, God wants to reveal His love *through* your life! Many times, we overcomplicate this idea by thinking public ministry—like teaching a class or serving in an orphanage—is the only way to fulfill that calling. However, I believe each of us finds incredible fulfillment when we allow God's love to flow through us in practical ways every day, touching the people around us.

It is all about proximity. We simply need to ask ourselves, *Who is in my life?*

You can be confident that God wants you to love and positively encourage everyone in your family—your husband, children, parents, siblings, and other extended family members.

We should ask ourselves, *How can I encourage those in my family with God's love?* As we look at each one and their unique situations, we might consider questions like:

♥ How can I encourage my mother-in-law as she struggles with the loneliness of retirement?

♥ How can I positively influence my daughter to be strong in the face of peer pressure?

♥ What is a practical way I can reveal God's love for my over-worked husband?

While we can be certain God wants us to minister to our families, we can also be confident that He wants us to positively influence other women! Each one of us shares the same call—to minister to the women in our lives.

I've been a part of church my entire life. And through the years I've received ample teaching and acquired a lot of head knowledge. But it wasn't until more spiritually mature women started speaking into my life in a personal way that I was able to apply the knowledge. Real-life change happened when women stepped into my life, connected with me emotionally, and helped me apply God's truth specifically to my situations.

Attending church services and participating in small groups were an important part of my spiritual journey. But my relational and emotional needs as a woman were met through a one-on-one approach to ministry.

Every one of us benefits from having many different types of relationships. While we can enjoy spending time with our peers, we can also learn by being with people who are more experienced than we are. We gain different perspectives by hanging out with people who are older and younger than we are. We become more compassionate when we have relationships with people who have special needs. And we can make a difference in someone's life when we connect with someone who has less experience than we do.

Ministry to women is relational. As we live in full devotion to God, He will give us opportunities to reveal His love in life-changing ways. The love of God can heal relationships, provide in times of need, and grant peace in the most difficult circumstances.

Who are the women God wants you to connect with—your co-worker, your neighbor, your hair stylist? It can be as simple as writing an encouraging note to a struggling friend, spending an hour getting to know someone's story, or helping an aging neighbor with a household task.

Know that God will reveal His love through you! You can make a difference in the lives of the women around you as you give them the simple gifts of presence, understanding, compassion, conversation, and example.

God has given you an assignment to relational ministry. As you allow God's love to flow through you, you will meet the needs of others and at the same time discover the fulfilling life you were intended to lead!

about the authors

Kerry Clarensau is a speaker, mentor, author, and inspiring leader of women. She has served in ministry with her husband, Mike, for over 20 years. Recently, they served as pastors of a culturally diverse church in Wichita, Kansas. She has served in a variety of ministry positions in the Kansas district of the Assemblies of God and the National Office. Previously, Kerry served as the National Girls Ministries director (formerly Missionettes) and as the Leadership Development Coordinator for the National Women's Department.

Kerry's honesty and wisdom have made her a well-loved contributor to publications such as *Today's Pentecostal Evangel, Leader's Touch, Enrichment Journal, All About Mom/Insights for Mom, and Side By Side.* Kerry is also the author of a Bible study for wives, *Secrets: Transforming Your Life and Marriage* (Gospel Publishing House, 2009). Check out her blog at secretsbiblestudy.com.

Kerry and Mike have two sons, Blake and Tyler, a daughter-in-law, Katie, and a granddaughter, Molly.

JoAnn Butrin is a missionary with the Assemblies of God World Missions. She began her missionary career serving as a registered nurse in a very rural hospital in northeast Zaire in the Ituri Forest. She observed the need for health education and public health as she saw the same preventable diseases returning to the clinics and hospital over and over. She spent fourteen years in that area of the world, now known as the Democratic Republic of Congo.

She earned her BS from Evangel University and a Master's Degree in Community Health from Penn State. She later earned the PhD from the University of Minnesota and a Certificate of Tropical Health from Tulane University. She then joined the staff of the Assemblies of God medical mission's arm, HealthCare Ministries, in 1987, later becoming the director. She has traveled to many countries of the world, with medical teams or as a speaker or lecturer.

She is now the director of International Ministries for the Assemblies of God World Missions. In all of her studies, she grew more and more convinced that a developmental holistic approach to health and missions was the most effective means of ministry. Dr. Butrin also has a keen interest in HIV/AIDS and has published several books and manuals on this topic. She directs an organization called the Global AIDS Partnership. She has lectured on Community Health and Development, HIV/AIDS, and teaches a course on social justice.

Jodi Detrick has a passion for writing in a way that makes biblical truths alive and accessible. She is a regular religion columnist for *The Seattle Times,* one of America's leading daily newspapers with an estimated total readership of 1.8 million. In that venue she has been able to address a large, mostly unchurched (and highly skeptical toward anything that smacks of "organized religion"), audience about issues of faith since 2007. In addition, her articles have been published in many different periodicals and books, as well as online e-zines.

A frequent retreat, conference, and special events speaker for many different groups and denominations across America, Jodi loves to talk to audiences at a heart level about things that matter most. She is convinced that when people encounter the living God through His Son, Jesus, they will be forever changed. She uses warmth, humor, and stories from real life to weave biblical messages with deep spiritual truths, trusting that, beyond what she can bring, "God *always* has something up His great big sleeve" for every group and event.

Another of Jodi's passions is being a personal and leadership coach who helps people get "unstuck" so they can make significant progress in their journey of life (www.significantlifecoaching.com). Jodi's own educational journey led her to seminary where she earned a Master's Degree and now she's finishing up a doctorate in leadership. But beyond any formal degrees or positions, being a wife, mother, and "Grammy" to her grandgirls have been her sweetest (sometimes hardest), and most rewarding roles.

Jodi currently serves as the Chairperson for the Network for Women in Ministry, a national network dedicated to developing, mentoring, resourcing, and supporting vocational and volunteer women in ministry and women preparing for ministry. A long-time pastor's wife, she also served as the Women's Ministries Director for the Northwest Ministry Network from 2001 to 2009. She loves to have meaningful conversations with people about things that count (preferably over a good cup of Starbucks) and is especially thrilled when she has the opportunity to mentor and influence younger women.

Jodi and her husband, Don, (who always cheers her on!) live in North Bend, Washington (near Seattle) where Don serves on the Northwest Ministry Network executive leadership team.

Janelle Hail is the founder of the National Breast Cancer Foundation.

At 34-years old, the mother of three was diagnosed with breast cancer, a disease that will affect more than 200,000 this year alone. At the time of her diagnosis, she was living a healthy lifestyle and had no family history of breast cancer.

From her personal experience and a compassionate heart to help others, Janelle's vision for the National Breast Cancer Foundation was formed. She strengthened her voice to reach women with lifesaving education on breast cancer by becoming a professional speaker and award-winning writer. In her pursuit of reaching out to women who have no assistance, Janelle has received numerous accolades on behalf of NBCF.

Today, Janelle serves as the CEO of National Breast Cancer Foundation, one of America's most highly recognized and respected breast cancer charities. To Janelle, nothing compares to the joy in life she receives when she hugs a woman whose life has been spared by a mammogram provided by the National Breast Cancer Foundation.

In 2010, Janelle celebrated her 30th year as a breast cancer survivor.

Joanna Weaver is known the world over for her transparent and life-changing books, *Having A Mary Heart in a Martha World and Having a Mary Spirit.* These two books have sold over a million copies and have been translated into several languages including Spanish, French, Dutch, Chinese, German, Korean, and more. Joanna has appeared on a wide variety of nationally syndicated radio and television broadcasts. Past appearances include: *The Harvest Show, At Home Live with Chuck & Jenni, Midday Connection, HomeWord, and Janet Parschall's America.* She is also a highly sought after speaker and shares her message at intimate gatherings and several high profile events each year. But Joanna's greatest joy is found in being a wife and mother and in her role as a pastor's wife.